Travel with Us

Our Family Vacation to Mexico

Written by 7 year old
Jaiyen L. Bhandari
(with help from some adults)

To request permission, contact the publisher at:
publisher@innerpeacepress.com

ISBN: 978-1-958150-65-8
Travel with Us: Our Family Vacation to Mexico

First edition: June 2025
Printed in U.S.A.

Published by Inner Peace Press
Eau Claire, Wisconsin
www.innerpeacepress.com

To Mama, thank you for inspiring me to write this book since you also write books about our family traditions.

To my Au Pair, Lina, thank you for helping me create and design this book, and for bringing my story to life.

Hi! My name is Jaiyen.
I am from the "Windy City," Chicago.

- CHICAGO -

I live with my mom. my dad.
and my little brother Kishyn.

I like basketball and playing outside
and I love living in Chicago.

Today is a special day!
It's my birthday!!

And we are going to
Mexico for Spring Break!

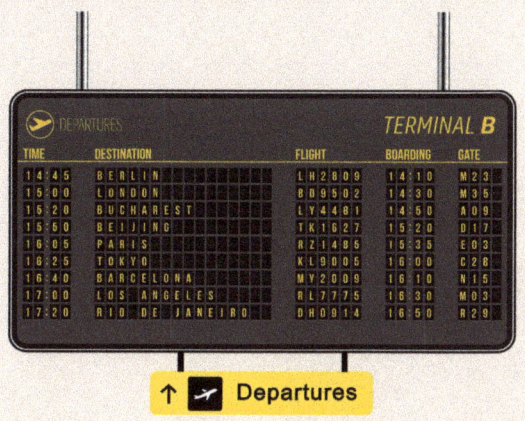

DEPARTURES

TERMINAL B

TIME	DESTINATION	FLIGHT	BOARDING	GATE
14:45	BERLIN	LH2809	14:10	M23
15:00	LONDON	BB9502	14:30	M35
15:20	BUCHAREST	LY4481	14:50	A09
15:50	BEIJING	TK1627	15:20	D17
16:05	PARIS	RZ1485	15:35	E03
16:25	TOKYO	KL9005	16:00	C28
16:40	BARCELONA	MY2009	16:10	N15
17:00	LOS ANGELES	RL7775	16:30	M03
17:20	RIO DE JANEIRO	DH0914	16:50	R29

↑ ✈ Departures

Early in the morning, we arrived at Chicago O'Hare Airport for our flight to Cancun, Mexico.

Cancun is located on the Yucatan Peninsula. A peninsula is a piece of land almost fully surrounded by water.

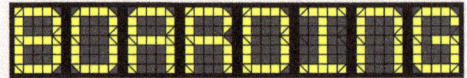

BOARDING

after 10 minutes

after 4 hours

Soon after checkin. we boarded our plane. We were patiently waiting for everyone to get on the plane. But instead of taking off. they told us to get OFF the plane. Our aircraft needed to get fixed.

We could not get back on the plane for 4 hours! It was a really long wait!

When we finally took off they said the flight
would be more than 3 hours long, so we watched
a movie on our tablets and then took a nap.

Before we landed, the flight attendant came over
and said "Happy Birthday" and gave me some
wings on a special pin I could wear. It made me
feel happy after the long day.

When we landed in Cancun, we went to baggage claim to get our luggage, and then headed outside.

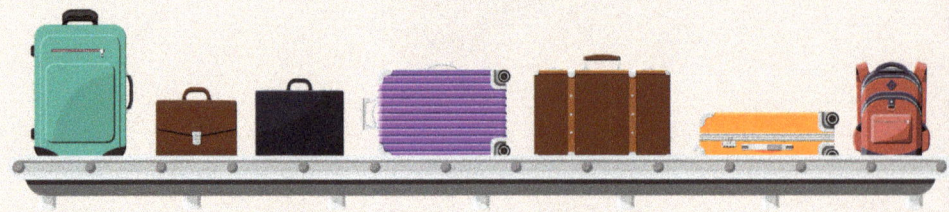

To get to our hotel we took a very special car service – in a sports car! This was not the usual way we travel, but my dad said it was for my special day.

When we arrived at the hotel, my brother and I played Legos while my parents unpacked the luggage.

Our hotel room had a room with a sofa and a bedroom with two beds next to it. Plus it had a big balcony with a view of the ocean!

After a while, we went down to the hotel lobby to meet up with some friends who also came to Mexico. They flew in from Detroit, Michigan, which is sort of close to Chicago but still pretty far away.

It makes me so happy that our families get to travel on Spring Break together every year.

More people equals more fun!

We were soooo hungry after waiting for our friends. We were lucky that there was a taco stand next to our hotel!

For lunch we had some yummy tacos. guacamole. and chips. I even got to have a little sweet soda because it we are on vacation.

With our bellies full we went back to the hotel
and changed into our swimsuits.

Then we FINALLY went to the beach.

We splashed in the water, but the waves were a
little scary. So, we spent most of our time
playing near the ocean in the sand.

We found some really cool seashells and started
to build a sand castle. While we were playing,
we saw fish jumping in the distance!

After time at the beach, we headed to the pool! My brother and I love swimming in a pool. This pool had a special "fishtank" section, which had a wall of glass, so you could see inside the pool from outside.

Check out the photo my mom took of me!

After a fun-filled day, we showered, changed, and went to dinner at a yummy restaurant, where they sang "happy birthday" to me in Spanish.

Afterwards, we had delicious ice cream, which is called helados in Spanish. My favorite flavor was chocolate!

It was a great first day. I was even more excited for the next day, because before bedtime my mom and dad said they had a special surprise planned.

I was so tired from all the fun we had and all the delicious food, that I fell asleep in 2 seconds flat!

The next day my family and our friends went on a boat ride! It was a little bit windy, but it was a lot of fun.

We sailed to a nearby island, where we explored the town and bought necklaces made with real shark's teeth!

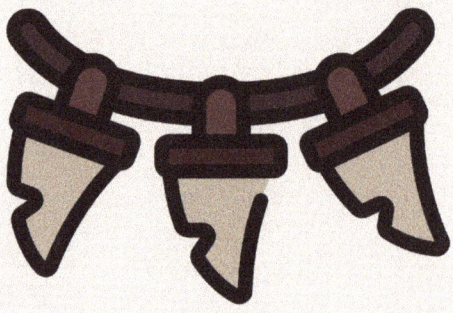

Then we went to a beach for some swimming, before walking back to the boat. During the boat ride home we saw a colorful sunset.

After the boat ride we had pizza at the hotel, and went back to our rooms for the night.

It was a fun and tiring day.

The next few days we went from the beach to the pool, and from the pool to the beach, over and over again.

We also spent time at the kids club. We met a lot of new friends there and got to play with toys and do fun activities.

It was a good way to "take a break" as my mom says.

On the last day, after a week of beach, pool, food, and friends, we ended our trip with a beautiful sunset walk on the boardwalk.

We would miss our friends a lot after this trip!

It is nice to know we would see them again at next spring break, and hopefully before.

The next day, it was time to
fly back home to Chicago.

I was thinking about all the fun we had on
the trip and I was sad to leave. But, I was
also glad to go home to my room, my toys,
and my friends in Chicago too.

Cancun,
Mexico

Chicago,
Illinois, USA

When we got home, Chicago was much colder than Mexico. We kept the sunshine going at home by crafting a picture frame with the seashells we found at the beach.

I had so much fun in Mexico.

Hope you enjoyed exploring with us!

Travel Guide for
MEXICO

WHAT WE PACKED

swim googles

sunblock

sunnies a.k.a.
sunglasses

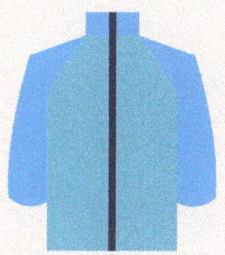

swimwear

pool toys

beach toys

flip flops/
sandals

hats

HISTORIC SITES
near Cancun

Chichen Itza- one of the "New 7 Wonders of the World"

Cenotes - Cave swimming holes common in Mexico

Tulum Ruins- Ancient ruins in the city of Tulum

Mexican
FOOD

Chips and Guacamole

Tacos

Burritos

Elotes

Churros

ABOUT THE AUTHOR

Jaiyen L. Bhandari

Jaiyen was born in Chicago to
American-Indian parents.
He has a little brother and a big,
extended family. He loves playing
basketball and tennis, spending time
with his family, and playing with
friends. He really loves living in Chicago.

Jaiyen's Mom inspired him to write
his own book because she recently
published some children's books (you
can find them on her website:
www.parullbhandari.com).

Jaiyen loves to travel to warm places,
preferably with a beach and a pool, so
he decided to write this book about his
trip to Cancun, Mexico.

MY TRAVEL SCRAPBOOK

DISCUSSION GUIDE

Some questions you can use to discuss this book.

1. Do you remember the name of the peninsula Jaiyen visited? Have you ever seen a peninsula?

2. What was the reason for the airplane's delay? What other reasons could cause a plane to be delayed?

3. Do you remember what helados means?

4. What is guacamole? Do you know what fruit it is made of?

5. Where would you look forward to going with your family or friends?